Chief Powhatan

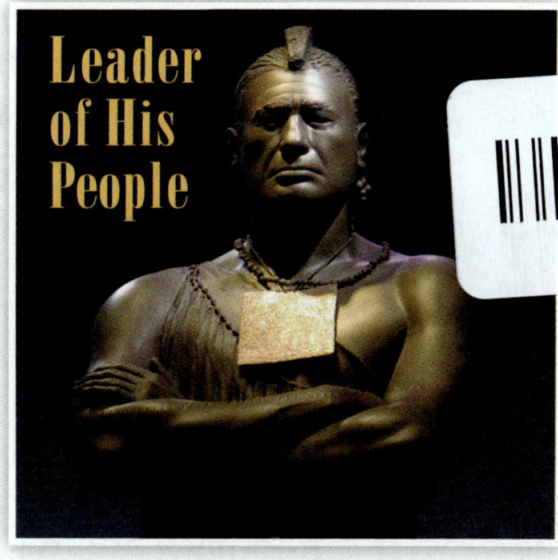

Susan Bachner

Boston, Massachusetts
Chandler, Arizona
Glenview, Illinois
Upper Saddle River, New Jersey

Illustrations
2, 3, 5, 6, 9, 10, 11, 13, 14, 15 Graham Kennedy.

Photographs
Every effort has been made to secure permission and provide appropriate credit for photographic material. The publisher deeply regrets any omission and pledges to correct errors called to its attention in subsequent editions.

Unless otherwise acknowledged, all photographs are the property of Pearson Education, Inc.

Photo locators denoted as follows: Top (T), Center (C), Bottom (B), Left (L), Right (R), Background (Bkgd)

Opener: ©Visions of America, LLC/Alamy; 1 ©Visions of America, LLC/Alamy; 4 ©Visions of America, LLC/Alamy; 7 Library of Congress; 8 ©Ilene MacDonald/Alamy; 12 Library of Congress.

ISBN-13: 978-0-328-67688-0
ISBN-10: 0-328-67688-8

3 4 5 6 V0FL 16 15 14 13 12

Powhatan, a Powerful Leader

The year was 1607. A huge **lodge** rose on the banks of the York River in what is now Virginia. Inside stood the most powerful leader within hundreds of miles. He was tall and about 60 years old. Around his broad shoulders he wore a cape made of raccoon skins. Long chains of pearls hung around his neck. Surrounding him were many loyal fighters and servants.

This was no ordinary leader. This was Powhatan, who ruled over thousands of people. Of all the Native American leaders living along the Atlantic Coast during the 1600s, Powhatan was perhaps the most powerful. Yet neither Powhatan nor his people knew that they would soon face major changes to their way of life. In fact, an entire continent was about to change. That spring, in 1607, the first permanent English settlers in the Americas were about to arrive.

Powhatan's Rise to Power

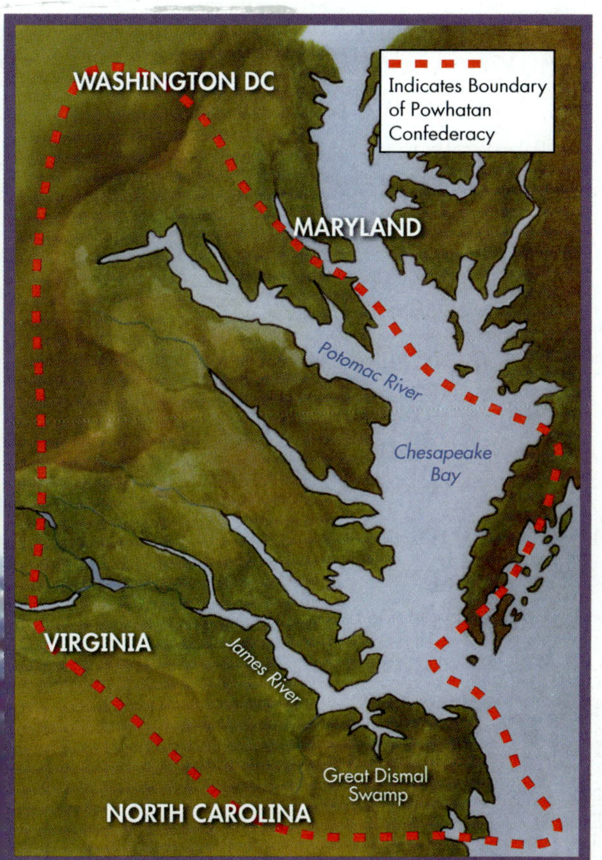

Chief Powhatan was born in the 1540s. His father had ruled in what is now Florida, but Spanish settlers had driven him and his people north. The Powhatan people settled in the area of modern Virginia. Here, Powhatan's father ruled over six Native American groups. Together, they formed the Powhatan **Confederacy**.

When Powhatan became chief, he wanted to expand the confederacy and bring more groups under his rule. He was able to succeed because of his skills as a leader and because his fighters were strong, smart, and courageous. They defeated many other Native American groups in the region. Some groups joined the confederacy out of fear. Others joined because Powhatan's people married husbands and wives from their groups.

By 1607, the Powhatan Confederacy covered land from the Potomac River to the Great Dismal Swamp. Powhatan is thought to have ruled about 30 different Native American groups and 20,000 to 30,000 people.

Powhatan and His People

The Powhatan people were highly skilled at farming, fishing, hunting, as well as making useful objects, such as tools, weapons, and bowls. To keep the soil **fertile** for farming, the Powhatan people made sure not to overuse their land. Every few years, they moved up or down the river valleys to new fields or to fields that had been unused for a while.

As chief, Powhatan demanded gifts from the people under his rule. His subjects brought him animal skins, beads, and other valuable items. They also gave him corn, turkeys, deer, and other foods. These gifts served as symbols of Powhatan's power, but they were useful, too. Not only did the gifts support Powhatan's family, they rewarded his chiefs and fed his fighters and servants.

How did Chief Powhatan keep his confederacy together? He replaced the chiefs of some groups with relatives. He also made sure that groups looked out for each other. Powhatan united them in order to fight enemies to the north and to the south. In this way, each individual group stayed safe and each group remained loyal to him. For many years, Powhatan carefully built his confederacy. He was the supreme leader and no one questioned him. Most people feared him. Now, all of that was about to change.

The English Arrive In Powhatan's Lands

In 1607, three ships from England sailed into Chesapeake Bay. The English ships, with their huge sails, were nothing like the dugout canoes used by the Powhatan people. However, these sailing ships were familiar to the Powhatans. Similar ships had sailed into Chesapeake Bay before and their crews had killed or kidnapped many Native American people.

The Powhatans watched as a group of settlers in small boats rowed to shore. The Powhatans forced the settlers to turn back and return to their ships. However, the English did not give up. They eventually made it to shore and built a fort there. They chose a place that was on a river, about 60 miles inland from the mouth of the bay. They named the river the James River, after their English king.

The English Settlers Meet Powhatan

A week after the Powhatans tried to chase away the settlers, some settlers took a boat up the river. They wanted to meet the people in the nearby villages. When they did meet Chief Powhatan, he was surrounded by his fighters and servants. The settlers were impressed by how Powhatan commanded **authority**. His people respected and feared him—and Powhatan expected the English to do the same.

Hard Times for Jamestown

The Jamestown settlers were not prepared to survive in the wilderness. Many of the settlers had been wealthy **gentlemen** in England who had paid others to do work for them. Even as Jamestown was being built, these men refused to do essential chores, such as chopping wood, collecting water, or planting seeds. Instead, they searched for gold. As a result, food became scarce soon after the settlers arrived.

When Powhatan's people visited the settlers' fort, they thought that many of the English settlers were lazy. Chief Powhatan realized that here was an opportunity to gain the upper hand. The English needed food. Powhatan and his people wanted the metal weapons, tools, and bowls that the English had. Powhatan offered to trade with the English. He even hoped he could convince them to join his confederacy. If he gained the support of the English—and their weapons—Powhatan could then attack his enemies and expand his great confederacy even more.

When the English came for food, they agreed to trade their copper bowls for corn and other supplies. They would not, however, part with their weapons. The English did not trust Powhatan, and he did not trust them.

Investing in Jamestown

The Virginia Company in England paid for the ships and supplies needed to start the Jamestown colony. Investors expected the settlers to find gold, silver, and other valuable metals and natural resources, such as timber, to send back to England.

An Uneasy Peace

Late in 1607, John Smith became one of the leaders of Jamestown. He wanted to set out and explore the area around the settlement as well as do more trading. Instead, Chief Powhatan's fighters captured Smith and brought him back to the main village.

When Smith later spoke about this event, he claimed that Powhatan sentenced him to death. Smith said that his head was placed on a stone, and some of Powhatan's fighters were about to kill him. Then, Smith said that Pocahontas, a young daughter of Powhatan, **intervened**. According to Smith, Pocahontas stopped her father from killing him since no one dared go against Powhatan's favorite daughter.

Today, many historians do not entirely believe Smith's story. They think that Powhatan set up a **ceremony** to adopt Smith. By having Pocahontas save Smith from death, Powhatan intended to bring Smith into his confederacy.

Powhatan now viewed Smith as a member of his people. Most likely, Powhatan assumed that the other English settlers would now be loyal to him, too. Finally, however, he let Smith return to Jamestown. For the time being, there was peace.

Jamestown buildings looked much like buildings in England.

The "Starving Time"

From 1608 to 1609, Smith ordered the English settlers to work hard. Smith didn't want Jamestown to have to depend on Powhatan. Still, for two years it was Chief Powhatan who prevented the settlers from going hungry. Sometimes, he gave them food; other times, he traded it. After two years, however, Powhatan grew frustrated with the English settlers' ongoing demands.

When John Smith returned to England in the fall of 1609, Powhatan decided to lay **siege** to Jamestown. He stopped providing food to the settlers and, instead, had fighters harass and attack them. Without Smith's leadership, the settlers stopped working. As a result, many of the settlers ended up dying from starvation or disease.

Chief Powhatan's plan almost succeeded. The few remaining settlers were ready to abandon Jamestown. Fortunately, in the spring of 1610, more ships and settlers arrived from England, bringing plenty of supplies. Jamestown would survive, but would Powhatan's confederacy?

All-Out War

Now, there were more English settlers in the Powhatan people's homeland than ever before. The English began to take over land that the Powhatan people farmed. The English also attacked several Powhatan villages. In one case, they destroyed an entire village and killed everyone, including children.

The English expected Powhatan and his people to go along with their demands for more land and food. Chief Powhatan, however, refused to give in to the English. Instead, his fighters attacked the settlers more often and captured some English weapons. Then, one event changed everything. In 1613, an English captain decided to kidnap one of Powhatan's children.

Powhatan's fighters watched as settlers carried supplies off their boats.

Pocahontas, Powhatan's Favorite Daughter

Chief Powhatan had many children. However, according to John Smith, Pocahontas was Powhatan's "most dear and well-beloved daughter." When she was young, Pocahontas often visited Jamestown. Her father sometimes sent her to deliver messages, or to help bring food and furs to trade for hatchets and other goods.

Powhatan had sent his favorite daughter on these trips as a sign of peace to the English settlers. Pocahontas moved easily between the two cultures. Now, however, she knew that her father saw the English as enemies. Yet, Pocahontas was still curious about them—and she fell right into the English captain's trap.

The English Kidnap Pocahontas

With the help of one of Pocahontas's friends, the English captain tricked Pocahontas into visiting his ship. Once Pocahontas was on board, he prevented her from leaving.

Pocahontas being captured by the settlers

The English held Pocahontas for ransom. In exchange for her safe return, they asked for corn and they demanded that Powhatan turn over all the weapons that he had captured. The English knew that having these weapons made Powhatan and his fighters stronger.

Chief Powhatan loved his daughter dearly and feared losing her. At the same time, Powhatan realized that without the weapons, his people could not defend themselves against the English. He made the decision not to turn over the weapons. Instead, he claimed that they had been stolen or were broken and useless.

The English did not believe Powhatan. They refused to let Pocahontas go, moving her from the ship to Jamestown. In Jamestown, Pocahontas dressed in English clothes and learned how to speak English. Months in Jamestown turned into a year. Pocahontas was not allowed to leave. She was starting to embrace her new life.

A Second Attempt at Peace

While in Jamestown, Pocahontas met a settler named John Rolfe who grew tobacco. He thought the settlers could make a great deal of money by **exporting** tobacco to England. In 1614, the settlers did just that. Soon, many people in England wanted to buy this Virginia tobacco.

Pocahontas Marries John Rolfe

Eventually, Pocahontas and Rolfe decided to marry and Chief Powhatan gave his consent. However, he didn't attend the ceremony. He refused to set foot in an English settlement.

The English were pleased with the marriage. Powhatan may have felt relief that Pocahontas would be safe now. However, his favorite daughter was giving up her culture to live with the English. For a time, the marriage of Pocahontas and Rolfe in 1614 led to a new period of peace called "The Peace of Pocahontas."

Before she married John Rolfe, Pocahontas converted to Christianity.

Tobacco, Then and Now

Tobacco had long been part of the culture of many Native American groups. It played a role in religious ceremonies and other important events. When the English settlers came and began growing tobacco, many of them mistakenly believed that it was good for one's health.

Today, we know that any use of tobacco is harmful. Tobacco is an addictive drug that can cause mouth cancer, lung cancer, and other deadly diseases.

The Trouble with Tobacco

Growing tobacco meant success for the Jamestown settlers. However, for the Powhatan people, tobacco meant more conflicts with the English. The settlers needed huge fields to grow tobacco, so they took over more and more of the Powhatan people's lands. Great numbers of settlers poured into the Virginia colony to grow tobacco with the hope of making a decent living or maybe even becoming wealthy.

As the English claimed more land, Powhatan's people were forced to move farther inland. They had to leave behind the river valleys where they had farmed and fished for as long as they could remember. Even Powhatan moved his lodge and main village to get far away from the English.

The Deaths of Pocahontas and Chief Powhatan

In 1616, Pocahontas, Rolfe, and their young son, Thomas, sailed to London with several Powhatans. Rolfe hoped to convince people in England to invest more money in Jamestown to keep the colony going strong. During this time of peace, he also hoped greater numbers of settlers would be willing to come to America.

After seven months in England, Rolfe decided to take his family back to Virginia. They set sail, but soon Pocahontas became too sick to travel. They returned to England, but not in time to cure her illness. Pocahontas was only about 21 years old when she died. The cause of death was, in all likelihood, pneumonia or another lung disease. Chief Powhatan had now lost his daughter forever.

Tired of the constant struggles with the English, Powhatan gave up most of his ruling powers. In 1618, just one year after Pocahontas died, Powhatan also died. He was about 70 years old.

The End of Chief Powhatan's World

The flood of settlers pouring into America proved too powerful even for Powhatan. He had hoped that the settler would unite with his people under his command, but they kept going to war instead.

After Powhatan's death, Powhatan's younger brother became the new chief. He was determined to go to war and push the settlers out. In the years that followed, thousands of the Powhatan people died. Some died in war while others died from diseases brought over by the English settlers. Forced from their hunting grounds and fertile farm lands, the Powhatans also suffered from severe food shortages. The struggle between the English and the Powhatan people for land and resources lasted for several decades.

Today, only a few of the Powhatan people still live on part of their homelands in Virginia. They have survived, passing on their traditions and their long history. They're working to keep their culture and the memory of their great leader, Powhatan, alive as part of the history of all Americans.

A boy keeps the Powhatan traditions alive.

Glossary

authority the power to decide what others may or may not do

ceremony a formal activity conducted for a specific purpose

confederacy groups of people who join together for some common purpose

export to send goods to another country for sale

fertile good for growing crops

gentlemen men born of high rank in England who were not used to doing physical work

intervene to come between people to stop a fight or argument

lodge a Native American dwelling or home.

seige encircling and blocking an enemy while attacking them